Text: Olivier Astruc
Photos: Philippe Poux
J-Paul Azam

CARCASSONNE

Historic City

Editions APA-POUX - ALBI
Collection As de Cœur

CARCASSONNE : A book of stones of many contradictory influences.

Over and above any historical influence, geographical factors are crucial in determining and shaping human settlement on a particular site. Even before it was a much coveted possession, the site of Carcassonne was naturally attractive. Its charm is vibrantly reflected in the words of the 19th century poet Gustave Nadaud :

I can see that here below on earth
No-one's happiness is complete.
My wish will have no worth :
I have never seen Carcassonne...
If I could only find two days
at Autumn's end
My God! I'd gladly die content
After having beheld Carcassonne...

But let's get back to the architectural essentials signed by Mother Nature, who patiently designed this curious environment, seemingly closed off to the outside world, yet wide open to contradictory external influences.

On the edge of a small sandstone plateau formed by a sudden meander of the Aude, the City overlooks the river-bend. Flowing down from the Pyrénées side, the south-north course of the river abruptly veers East in search of the Great Blue sea. It is here also, that we encounter the much straighter line (a human construction in this instance), of the Canal du Midi - a unique and genial aquatic link between the Atlantic and Mediterranean.

Although the site of Carcassone is relatively elevated, rising proudly erect from a setting of vineyards and emphasised by the vertical lines of its church spires, we do not lose sight of the nearby massive mountain frontiers : to the south, the first slopes of the Corbières mountains, dominated by the shimmering, lacy crags of the Pyrénées. To the north, the dark wooded horizon of the Montagne Noire. It is precisely at the crossroads of this vast land of mineral giants, that the stunning city of Carcassonne has always been a link between two regions placed back to back : the Atlantic and the Mediterranean.

Steeped in History, imprinted with remarkable events, Carcassonne has been an inspiration to many artists - Michel Sardou's heartfelt lyrics from 1979 are a typical example :

> *"....If I could have chosen my place of birth,*
> *Where I'd spend my life as a man,*
> *I would surely have chosen first,*
> *Beneath the ramparts of Carcassonne..."*

Now you just have to leaf through this fabulous book of stones, whose historic pages are filled with turbulent memories and dreams come true. With the passing of centuries, the hand of man has slowly but effectively shaped a "whim of the gods".

VUE DE CARCASSONNE.

A conflicting succession of invasions and feudal powers

The first historic evidence of Carcassonne City can be traced far back to the beginning of the 8th century BC. It was a simple oppidum (pre-Roman enclosed town) surrounded by an earthern wall, situated 2 km to the south-west on the heights of Mayreville, overlooking the Aude river. Two hundred years later, the small fortress was replaced by a cattle pen and the human habitat was moved to the present site of the City, sheltered by modest fortifications. Occupied by a Celtic tribe, the Tectosage Volques, it was named Carcasso.

One hundred and eighteen years before Jesus Christ, new conquerers, the Romans, came from the south, creating Narbonne province and building a Gallo-Roman city wall, whose vestiges can still be seen. The first upheaval occurred in the 5th century AD with the invasion by the Visigoths, who kept control of the city for three hundred years. Carcasso became Carcassona.

Then the Arab occupation began towards 725 and gave birth to the famous legend of Dame Carcas during an historic siege. 34 years later however, Pepin le Bref's army of Franks took hold of the city until the dissolution of the Frank empire. Feudalism followed, ruled by three dynasties of counts : the Olibas and Arsendes, the Arnauds, Rogers and Ermengardes and finally, the Trencavels.

Troubled times began again with the siege of Carcassonne from the 1st to the 15th August 1209, during the Albigenses crusade. Here are a few extracts recounted by the historian Dovetto :

"After having massacred the inhabitants and pillaged the town of Béziers on the 22nd July 1209, the Crusaders reached Carcassonne on the 1st of August...On the 3rd of August, they launched an assault on St Vincent just to the north. After an heroic resistance by Trencavel and his men, the town fell to the assailants, who then set fire to it. The Crusaders progressed south-west to the foot of the hill and set up camp between the Aude and the City, preventing the beseiged from gaining access to the river water... On the 7th of August, the siegers attacked the Castellar but were stopped by the determined resistance of the Carcassonne inhabitants.

On the 8th of August, an opening made in the City wall enabled the Crusaders to take the outer city. After a gruelling combat in the torrid August heat, the defendants were left exhausted and suffering terribly from thirst and dysentry.

Raymond-Roger de Trencavel had to resign himself to negotiating a surrender that he hoped could still be honourable. Once in the Crusader's camp however, he was taken prisoner. Deprived of their lord, the citizens opened the gates of the city to the French, who expelled them and seized hold of the city's enormous wealth. Another version claims that the Crusaders entered a city deserted of its inhabitants, who had all fled to Cabaret castle through underground tunnels.

On the 15th of August 1209, Simon de Montfort was proclaimed Count of Carcassonne by Pope Arnaud Amalric's legate. The unfortunate Viscount Raymond-Roger de Trencavel died on the 10th of November 1209, a prisoner of Simon in his own castle".

Simon the conquerer was to continue his destructive campaign throughout the entire region before attacking the County of Toulouse, where he was killed during the 1218 siege. His son, Amaury de Montfort finally relinquished his hold on the Viscounty of Carcassonne and it was attached to the French Crown in 1226.

Raymond Trencavel makes an unsuccessful attempt to reconquer the City.

The unfortunate destiny of Raymond-Roger de Trencavel however, left a deep and bitter imprint, which pushed his son, Raymond Trencavel to attempt to win back his ancestral fief in a disasterously unsuccessful siege. An extract from Seneschal Guillaume des Ormes' report to Queen Blanche de Castille on the 13th October 1240 gives us an idea :

"Your Excellency, should know that Viscount Trencavel set siege to Carcassonne on the 1st of September 1240...We took the woods in the outskirts of the city at Graveillant and this was good for us. The same day, the enemy captured a mill from us....On the other side, between the bridge and the castle barbican, there were many enemy soldiers stationed with so many crossbowmen that no-one could leave the city.

They then began to undermine the barbican at Narbonnaise gate; we countered them and erected a large, strong wall of dry stones so that we were able to keep control of the remaining section of the barbican, the other part having collapsed.

One Sunday, they assembled all their armed men, crossbowmen and others and together they attacked the barbican above the castle... We went to the barbican and threw so many stones and shot so many arrows at them that they were forced to abandon the assault. On Monday the 11th of October, towards evening, they heard rumours that your people, Madame, were coming to help us, so they set fire to the houses in the outer city...All of those who were taking part in the so-called siege furtively abandoned it that night...During the siege, none of our men wanted for food....we had abundant wheat and meat, enough for a long wait..."

The outcome of this abortive attempt was that Raymond Trencavel gave up the Viscounty of Car-

cassonne once and for all, to the King of France, in 1246..

A year later and until 1260, the "ville basse" or lower part of the city was to develop, since most of the administrative, political and religious activities now took place here instead of in the upper City.

It is no hazard then, that at the beginning of the Hundred Years War in 1335, Prince Edward of Wales, better known as the notorious Black Prince, destroyed the lower city but spared the old upper City.

During the turbulence of the Religious Wars in the 16th and 17th centuries, Carcassonne remained loyal to royalty and the Catholic church. The French Revolution was to bring further trouble : in 1793, a large quantity of archives was unfortunately burnt; the castle chapel, the parish church of Saint Sernin and the abbey of the Canons of Saint-Nazaire were destroyed, whereas the cathedral was spared...to be used as a hay store for the army !

A heritage that was plundered.....then stunningly restored by Viollet le Duc

Until the 17th century, Carcassonne was a strategically important city on the border between the French and Spanish kingdoms. As soon as Roussillon was taken back by the Crown in 1659, the border was not so close and the City's imposing fortifications lost much of their strategic importance. Rapidly, the residents of the city began to tear them down and recuperate the historic masonry to use for house building.

This sombre episode is recounted by Mr Dovetto of the Historical Monuments Society : "In the 19th century, the City was to disappear, as tower by tower and wall by wall, it was sold for its stones. (This was how the Aude barbican came to be demolished in 1816).

Fortunately, a local historian, Jean-Pierre Cros-Mayrevieille and the writer, Prosper Mérimée were to use their influence with parliamentarians and Prince Louis Napoléon Bonaparte, to obtain financial aid for the restoration of the city.

The great architect, Viollet le Duc (1841-1879) was given the responsibility of the salvage work that was to continue almost without interruption from 1852 to 1910; the final touches were completed by the architect, Boeswilldwal after 1879. Restoration was concentrated mainly on the rebuilding of crenellations along the walls and certain towers, as well as re-roofing. As this represented about 10% of the total volume of masonry, fortunately restoration was begun in time."

Due to the accomplishment of this monumental task, Carcassonne is proudly on display to visitors from all over the world - a stunning body of Middle Age fortifications, unique in Western Europe - a thousand years of military architecture.

Four great periods of military architecture, from the 4th to the 14th century.

■ Low-Empire : in the 4th century, the Gallo-Romans built a city wall that more or less follows the layout of the present wall. About one third of the initial length of the wall and a few of its towers have been preserved. The Gallo-Roman fortification is characterised by the use of small stones incorporating layers of red brick. The towers are placed at intervals of about 15 metres and are flat towards the interior of the square, and round towards the exterior, which faces the country. The window and door arches are brick-lined.

■ Feudal period : During the 12th century and at the very beginning of the 13th century, the powerful Trencavel viscounts, lords of Béziers and Carcassonne, built the castle (or fortress) in the city at the highest point on the hill. Repair work was also carried out on the unique city wall, which had been conserved from Gallo-Roman times and was still in use. Covering a vast quadrilateral of 80 X 40 metres, the fortress contained the Counts' palace and was isolated from the town by a moat.

■ The mid-13th century : After the bloody Crusade against the Albigenses (1209) and the annexation of the Viscounty of Carcassonne (1226), Blanche de Castille and Saint Louis had the outer city wall built : this new rampart completely enveloped the Gallo-Roman wall, protecting it and enabling work to be done on the old 4th century fortification, which was decrepit and unadapted to defence needs.

■ The late 13th century : Sheltered by the external wall that his father, Louis 9th, had just completed, Philippe III Le Hardi began the reconstruction of the Gallo-Roman wall. He was to pull down or reconstruct more than two-thirds of the 4th century ramparts. The resulting magnificent construction with its towers and formidable walls is characterised by the use of bossage stones. Military architecture was at its height in this period and each tower is in itself, an impregnable bastion.

At the beginning of the14th century, the restoration of Carcassonne City was completed. Nothing significant from a defence point of view was added after this period.

The "Mortes-Payes" defence corps.

Throughout the course of history the City of Carcassonne had always had a defensive vocation, to protect itself from outside attacks and invasions. The various stages of fortification that we have just described illustrate how the site was progressively better kept secure. To complete the security adequately and prevent invasion however, a human element in the form of a large body of soldiers was needed. This is why Saint Louis decided to set up a system of "Mortes-Payes", to "guard the City night and day...because of its proximity to Spain on the Roussillon side".

He took inspiration from a custom imposed in 1124 by Viscount Bernard Aton on his vassals, by the name of "devoir d'estage". The vassals were obliged to maintain a garrison of guards living on the spot with their families, at the vassal's own expense. The title of Morte-Paye was hereditary, included tax exemption and the guards were part of a garrison of 220 men responsible for permanent surveillance. In 1418, their numbers were halved but the duty was still as demanding and minutely programmed. The following extract gives an idea of the harsh conditions : "40 men, six of them trumpeters, took their turn on watch one night out of three. Two trumpeters went to the Narbonnaise gate to ensure the summons. Eighteen men and four trumpeters posted themselves along the inner wall, armed with swords and crossbows - one trumpeter was posted at each cardinal point.

The watch lasted all night without replacement. The other men in groups of eight walked the rounds of the lists and the high wall : twelve rounds in winter and six in summer. The trumpets at the cardinal points were sounded four times nightly in winter, three in summer. Duty was exhausting and the discipline extremely rigorous. Any man who abandoned his post, even to put out a fire in his own home, could be punished with death !" The Mortes-Payes guards were maintained until the French Revolution and they continued to watch over the city and keep the peace "intra muros".

Nowadays, law and order is ensured by the regular police force who carries out its work in less exacting conditions than the former peace-keepers !

Porte Narbonnaise city gate, an archetype of 13th century defence construction

Given this name because it faces East towards Narbonne, Porte Narbonnaise is the main entrance to the old City and leads directly to Comtal castle via rue Cros-Mayrevieille. The visitor goes into the city through a small stone castle containing a double draw-bridge, overlooking a wide moat and flanked by Saint Louis barbican.

This first defence post gives access to two huge twin towers, 25 metres high (excluding the roof) and 4 metres thick at their base. Built around 1280 under Philippe le Hardi, with bossage stones to ward off projectiles, they frame the access gate to the City, protected by a highly effective 13th century defence mechanism.

To check the enemy arriving from the outside, there was an anti-cavalry chain between the two towers that prevented men on horseback from getting any further. Against assailants on foot, the vault in the city access corridor was defended by a

machicolation, a portcullis of iron and wood whose slots can still be seen on the walls, as well as an enormous double-sided door fitted with two large bars. In case the enemy succeeded in crossing the first two defence barriers, the centre of the vault in the corridor was equipped with a huge clubbing device; a trapdoor from which the intruders were bombarded with all sorts of projectiles, even boiling oil. If by miracle, the enemy got past these obstacles, it was faced with yet another internal defence mechanism : machicolation, portcullis, gate locked and secured by two bars and archers on either side able to shoot at point blank range.

This made getting into the city somewhat difficult ! We can understand why the Black Prince left the upper City and its fortress alone, when he attacked the lower city in 1355. Even though it had been conquered in the past, from the 13th century on, the City was reputed so invincible that it was familiarly named "the virgin maid of Languedoc" !

The legend of Dame Carcas

In the 13th century during Arab occupation of the City, Dame Carcas, a Saracen princess was defending Carcassonne against Charlemagne and his army. The siege had lasted 5 years and inside the fortress, food was becoming scarce. Before coming to a decision, Dame Carcas had the houses of the city searched to gather up all possible remaining food. The soldiers brought back only a miserable sack of wheat and...a pig that an old woman had hidden in the depths of her cellar. The princess knew that it was useless to distribute these meagre rations to the garrison and the inhabitants - there would hardly be a mouthful for each person. Moreover, the soldiers being Muslims were not pork eaters. She force-fed the pig with the wheat and had it thrown from the top of the ramparts. The animal fell to the ground and split open, scattering all the wheat it had eaten before the astonished Charlemagne, who exclaimed :

Photo left page : Narbonnaise and Tréseau towers protecting the draw-bridge.

" If the Arabs can afford to throw their food "out of the window", then there must still be plenty of food in the city - useless to continue a siege that has already lasted so long".

The order was immediately given to raise the siege and to return home to France.

But Dame Carcas was a lady and was much more able to resist a siege than the charms of the handsomely bearded Emperor! As she watched Charlemagne riding away, she was overcome with a strange sadness at the thought of never seeing him again. She called him back, rang the church bells...and gave up her city to the tolling of all the city bells.

Since that day, it has been said that CARCAS...SONNE...(Charlemagne). (Carcas... rings... Charlemagne).

The great Emperor gave Dame Carcas in marriage to one of his faithful companions, Roger and the union was to produce the famous Trencavel dynasty.

Château Comtal
a stronghold within the fortress

A veritable camp entrenched within the City's fortifications, Château Comtal was built in the highest part of the city, as far away as possible from the main entrance of Porte Narbonnaise. Successive excavations have revealed that the fortress was erected on Gallo-Roman and Feudal remains.

Built in the 12th century by the Trencavel viscounts, the castle defences were reinforced in the reign of Saint Louis, notably the keep and the south wing, which were both raised. The buildings are set out in an imposing quadrilateral of eighty-four by forty metres, isolated from the rest of the city by a deep trench or moat, with an eighteenth century bridge. Like Porte Narbonnaise gate, the entrance is guarded by imposing twin towers framing the central defence corps.

In 1902, a tower and two curtains were equipped with wooden balconies, imitations of 12th century hoardings. These temporary installations were set up when the fortress was threatened and were used by two types of defence corps : the bombarders, who threw all sorts of projectiles onto the assailants through a system of open trapdoors overlooking the base of the walls; the archers who fired through the narrow horizontal slits of the loopholes.

The rectangular wall of Château Comtal was flanked with nine observation and defence towers. Six of them were built on more or less the same model : the two entrance towers, the Casernes, Major, Degré and Saint Paul

Château Comtal

towers. Of the other three, Pinte tower is probably the oldest of the castle and was built in two stages at the beginning of the 12th century. La Chapelle tower was rebuilt in the 13th century in the original Gallo-Roman style and La Poudre tower is from the Saint Louis period.

Inside the formidably defended fortress, the buildings were set around a large court of honour in the centre of which grew a stately elm in the Middle Ages - a symbol of nobility all over Languedoc. A second door opening to the west enabled access to the Aude river by way of the Aude barbican. The Counts' palace covered the three facades overlooking the court of honour. It was composed of the main body on the western side ajoining the defence wall, the south wing containing the great hall, the north wing, occupied by the chapel and destroyed during the French Revolution.

As for the habitat within this huge body of buildings, the Counts' lodgings were mainly on the first floors, whereas the storage area, kitchens, garrison, prison etc, were situated on the ground floor and in the cellars. To complete the scene in Medieval times, galleries and annex buildings, mainly wooden, were erected along the walls of the interior courtyard.

A visit to the impressive Château Comtal should also include a trip to the remarkable lapidary museum, divided into six periods : the Roman and Gallo-Roman room (sarcophaghi, tombstones, amphorae, oil grinding stones etc); the Roman room (capitals, modillions, ablution bowls, discoidal stones etc); the Round chamber in the keep with its mural paintings of battle scenes and a 15th century sandstone Calvary cross; the Gothic room with its tombstones, recumbant knight, 14th century Gothic windows, a white marble virgin and a curious crucifixion of Saint Pierre with the head facing down. The fifth room contains various corbels and capitals,

In the Chamber of the Counts, a late 15th century Calvary cross.

In Room N° 4, 14th century Gothic windows

polychrome alabasters, three altar tables, an entombment and a 13th century engraved brass platter. Finally, the last room is mainly an exhibition of the restoration of the City by Viollet le Duc. Overall, the museum is a fantastic trip through time recounting the incredible diversity of the City's history.

Porte d'Aude gate dominated by Tour de l'Inquisition and Tour Carré de l'Evêque towers.

The City walls and the Lists, a masterpiece of military architecture.

The huge Narbonnaise towers, the curtain and the massive Tréseau tower make up the formidable Eastern facade of the City.

Built in the 13th century by Saint Louis' son, Philippe III le Hardi, the towers are equipped with fireplaces, ovens, two water tanks of 20 000 litres and a salting vat that could contain meat from 100 oxen and 1000 pigs.

From Moulin du Connétable tower onwards, the Gallo-Roman wall is the best preserved of this period and was used as the only rampart until the mid-13th century. After Bérard and Moreti towers, the Gallo-Roman building style reappears in Marquière, Samson, Avar and Charpentière towers. Moulin du Connétable and Vieulas towers lean slightly forward and were restored by the 12th century viscounts, whereas the curtain up to Marquière tower was largely restored in the 13th century.

In this section, the outer wall is flanked by Notre Dame barbican, defending Amandiers postern (discreet exit door), which gave access to the lower town via Trivalle moat. Opposite the outer tower of Porte Rouge, Charpentière tower was named for its proximity to the old royal carpenter's workshop.

The approach to Château Comtal was carefully designed to slow down enemy progress towards the western door, hidden behind La Poudre and La Chapelle towers. The chicanes along the path for example, were a hinderance and assailants also had to pass beneath a wooden floor with trapdoors through which they were bombard-

ed with projectiles. As well, a narrow door near Pinte tower (also called Paon tower), hampered circulation along the lists. This is the oldest tower of the fortress. The western facade bears traces of the various periods of construction and features Romanesque, Gothic and even Renaissance windows.

As we continue on the path around the City, the lists are again bordered by the inner wall when we come to La Justice tower, which dates from Saint Louis' time and probably replaced a Gallo-Roman edifice. This tower defended the access to Porte d'Aude gate, facing West and was supplemented by a machicolation. A paved ramp between the two walls crosses over Sénéchal alley and then leads to the narrowest part of the lists with its two "bottlenecks", Petit and Grand Canissou, and Four Saint-Nazaire tower, a Gallo-Roman construction.

In this same section, Inquisition tower was reserved for the Bishop's use. His palace was situated just behind Tour Carré de l'Evêque tower, straddling the lists and forming a junction between the two city walls. Several other towers follow : Cahuzac, Mipadre and Moulin du Midi and all three were built by Philippe le Hardi to ensure the defence of the southern part of the City. It is in this triangle that the most furious battles took place during the 1240 siege. This is also the spot chosen to set up the open air theatre where in summer, spectacular reconstructions of Carcassonne's dramatic history are held for the public.

Opposite Mipadre tower and set into the outer defence wall, Grand Burlats tower stands out as a large edifice marking the extreme end of the citadel. Nearby are the ruins of a section of the Gallo-

Roman wall that was pulled down. Following the outer ramparts, Ourliac tower is smaller in comparison with Moulin du Midi tower, which leads us to the inner wall. Protected by Razès postern, Saint Nazaire tower, square in shape, enables a perpendicular entrrance to the curtain on the south side of the City. It is also protected by nearby Saint Martin tower, which covers the access to Razès door from another angle.

After passing the medium-sized Prisons, Casteras and Plô towers, the visitor comes to Balthazar tower, built on the ruins of Gallo-Roman walls. Opposite, a magnificent round tower, La Vade, is the largest and most beautiful of the outer wall. Like a sentinel watching over the entire south-eastern section of the City, it was built in Saint Louis' time and became the general quarters of the Mortes Payes guards, described earlier. At the top of the tower, a brightly painted wooden bird, the Papegay, was used as a target during archery contests to elect the king of the archers.

Though La Peyre tower is relatively small, it played an important role in defence, situated near the draw-bridge at the main entrance. It was also linked to bothTrauquet tower and Narbonnaise gate by an underground passage. An adjoining rectangular building from the Saint Louis period prolonged the access to the inside of the City.

As we come to Saint Sernin, a Gallo-Roman tower, we have now completed the rounds of the lists of Carcassonne. Featuring a flamboyant Gothic window added in the 15th century, it was used as the chevet for the parish church of the same name. It is in this tower that Saint Sernin was supposedly imprisoned in the 3rd century... before being miraculously released by a troop of angels - in a "celestial apparition"!

In short, at the end of such a stunning trip around the magnificently preserved lists, it seems obvious that the City of Carcassonne, with a defence system highly adapted to its environment, forms a veritable masterpiece of military architecture. With three kilometres of defence walls flanked by fifty-two towers and barbicans, we are in the heart of an exceptionally fascinating and unique site.

Representation of
Simon de Montfort
1150 - 1218

Vade or Papegay tower, like a sentinel watching over the south-east.

Eastern sector of the City, altered over the different periods.

The Cross at Porte d'Aude gate.

Following pages : Porte d'Aude gate and Château Comtal

Saint Nazaire south transept, Gothic apse, crenelated Romanesque belltower.

Saint Nazaire basilica, a combination of Romanesque and Gothic art.

With its Romanesque nave and Gothic transept, the City's basilica seems to reflect the long history of combined southern and northern influences. The basilicas's official name of Saint Nazaire et Celse is in itself an indication of its rather unusual dual character. The legend recounts that Nazaire, the son of Jewish and Christian parents, had to flee from Italy into Gaul. He was captured however and as a child by the name of Celse was crying when the arrest took place, the soldiers forced the child to follow them. When Neron saw the two prisoners, he had them thrown into a dungeon. Subsequently, a multitude of wild animals invaded Neron's gardens and tore almost everyone apart. The two captives then took refuge in Milan before being captured again and decapitated - a fate which often led to the canonisation of martyrs.

The basilica we admire today is composed of a Romanesque nave, began in 1096 and raised during the 12th century. The Gothic transept and choir were erected on the site of Romanesque apses between 1269 and the first third of the 14th century. Outside, the elegant edifice features polygonal bell-turrets, gargoyles, balustrades and huge stained glass windows.

The Romanesque nave is supported by a row of alternately square and round pillars, whereas the sculpture on the capitals is purely ornamental : stylised floral clusters or simple geometric shapes. In the Gothic transept and apse, the austere western wall contrasts with and highlights the luminous eastern facade, as the sun shines into the six chapels at the front. Tall, slender columns separate the chapels,

Following page : North transept, rose window of the Virgin.

South rose window, dedicated to Christ.

Alabaster recumbant bishop (15th century).

creating a breathtaking impression of lightness and elegance, which is replicated in the choir of the basilica with its twelve lofty pillars supporting fine Gothic vaulting. Such splendour and harmony is a tribute to the architects who managed to blend Romanesque sobriety with Gothic pomposity in an unlikely and rare balance of such different styles. You do not have to be a fervent Catholic to appreciate this wonderful edifice of thousand year old stones and timeless radiance.

It is worth mentioning that this marvel of religious architecture in the heart of the fascinating City of Carcassonne also shelters precious "gems" : Radulphe chapel contains the magnificent tomb of a bishop who died in 1206. There is a remarkable 17th and 18th century organ case, a First Empire gilded rostrum and a 16th century polychrome Pieta. Above all, this fantastic "book of stones" cannot be closed without a visit to the tombstone of the sinister Simon de Montfort, whose life-sized likeness is engraved in a great flagstone of pink marble, as well as a look at the curious bas-relief depicting the siege of a 13th century fortified town.

To finish on a more peaceful note, it is easily observed today, that the numerous "assailants" of the legendary City, far from seeking conflict, come to give tribute to its timeless and exceptional charm.

The poet Gustave Nadaud was certainly right when he readily proclaimed :

"My God !
I will die content
After having beheld Carcassonne."

13th century stone bas-relief depicting a siege.

17th and 18th century organs.

La Légende de Dame Carcas

Back cover :
Miniature illumination : "Carcassonne, storming of the outer town, 1209" - *Georges Delcausse*